Markus Hoffmann

Aus der Reihe: e-fellows.net stipendiaten-wissen

e-fellows.net (Hrsg.)

Band 672

Mergers and Acquisitions Motive

Overview of different types and objectives of M & A transactions and motives

GRIN Verlag

Bibliografische Information der Deutschen Nationalbibliothek:

Die Deutsche Bibliothek verzeichnet diese Publikation in der Deutschen Nationalbibliografie; detaillierte bibliografische Daten sind im Internet über http://dnb.d-nb.de/ abrufbar.

Imprint:

Druck und Bindung: Books on Demand GmbH, Norderstedt Germany
ISBN: 978-3-656-39237-8

This book at GRIN:

http://www.grin.com/en/e-book/210976/mergers-and-acquisitions-motive

Mergers and Acquisitions Motive

BACHELOR THESIS I

Bachelor Program

"Management and Law"

Management Center Innsbruck

Submitted by:

Markus Hoffmann

Hand in Date:

January 31, 2013

Content

Content I

Figures II

Abbreviations III

1 Introduction 1

1.1 Problem Statement 1

1.2 Objective 1

1.3 Procedural Method 2

2 Mergers and Acquisitions 3

2.1 History of Mergers and Acquisitions 3

2.2 Definition of Mergers and Acquisitions 4

2.3 Types of Mergers and Acquisitions 5

2.4 Objectives of Mergers and Acquisitions 7

3 Motives for Engaging in M & A Activity 8

3.1 Planning M & A Activity 8

3.2 Distinction of M & A Motives by their Effect on Shareholder Value 9

3.2.1 Motives that increase Shareholder Value 10

3.2.1.1 Synergy 10

3.2.1.2 Economies of Scale or Scope 12

3.2.1.3 Increased Market Power and Growth 13

3.2.1.4 Managerial Efficiency 13

3.2.2 Motives that decrease Shareholder Value 14

3.2.2.1 Managerial Hubris 14

3.2.2.2 Agency Problems 14

3.2.2.3 Free Cash Flow Theory 15

3.2.3 Motives with uncertain impact on Shareholder Value 15

4 Summary and How to Make M & A Transactions Successful 17

References 20

Figures

Figure 1: Announced Mergers & Acquisitions Worldwide 1985-2012. 4

Abbreviations

e.g.	example given
IT	Information Technology
M & A	Mergers and Acquisitions
p.	Page
R & D	Research and Development
US	United States of America
USD	United States Dollar

1 Introduction

1.1 Problem Statement

Mergers and acquisitions (M & A) are a form of corporate expansion and growth. They are not the only means of growth for a company, but they are an alternative to growth by internal or organic capital investments. (Sudarsanam, (1995) p. 1) The first decade of the new millennium was an era of global mega-mergers. Several factors like readily available credit, low interest rates, technological change and global competition fueled M & A activity and in 2007, M & A transactions reached a new record dollar volume worldwide. (DePamphilis, (2011) p. 13-14)

Mergers and acquisitions are an important means of removing underperforming managers or companies and transferring resources to where they are most needed. (DePamphilis, (2011) p. 124) However, there is considerable evidence that many M & A activities remain unsuccessful. Estimated failure rates are typically between 60 and 80 percent. (Homburg and Bucerius, (2006) p. 347)

1.2 Objective

Due to these high failure rates, it seems unreasonable for a company to engage in an M & A transaction, but still, more and more companies decide to do exactly that.

The goal of this paper is to give a structured overview of the different types and objectives of M & A transactions and the motives, which may lead companies to engage in those transactions.

Given the high failure rates of mergers and acquisitions, this topic is one that is of high significance and has been extensively researched in the past. This paper aims to collect the most important research that has been done on the topic of M & A motive, structure it and emphasize crucial findings.

1.3 Procedural Method

The first part of this paper introduces the reader to the world of mergers and acquisitions. After defining mergers and acquisitions, a brief overview of the various types and objectives is given. The next part of the paper informs the reader about the different motives, which may lead executives to engage in M & A transactions. Because shareholder value is essential to almost all firms, it is drawn upon as a framework to organize M & A motives in this paper. The last chapter of this paper summarizes the most important points and emphasizes some of the most crucial factors that make M & A transactions successful. This paper relies on literature study and research and is not empirical.

2 Mergers and Acquisitions

2.1 History of Mergers and Acquisitions

Businesses come and go over the years, probably best illustrated by the annual Fortune 500 list, a list of the 500 largest United States (US) corporations. Only 70 firms from the original 1955 list are still on the list in 2011 and about 2000 firms have appeared on the list at some point. Most companies disappear from the list through mergers, acquisitions, bankruptcy or downsizing. The general media uses the term *"Corporate Restructuring"* to describe actions taken to expand or contract a firms operations or to fundamentally change its structure. (DePamphilis, (2011) p. 4-5)

Like many other phenomena in business, mergers and acquisitions are subject to cyclical changes, so called "M & A waves". Those waves can be relevant for companies interested in engaging in the M & A market, because knowing the current state of a cycle allows companies to act anti-cyclical, thus potentially reducing costs. (Kummer, Eiffe, Mölzer, (2011), p. 3)

The first M & A wave took place during the time of industrialization in the early 1900s (Kummer, Eiffe, Mölzer, (2011), p. 3), and M & A transactions grew larger over time as shown in Figure 1. The 6th wave, which lasted from 2003 to 2008, lead to a new record volume of 4,063 billion US Dollars (USD) in M & A transactions in 2007. This wave was characterized by a very intense globalization of companies as well as by booming international capital markets, which made large cash transactions possible. (Picot, (2008) p. 4)

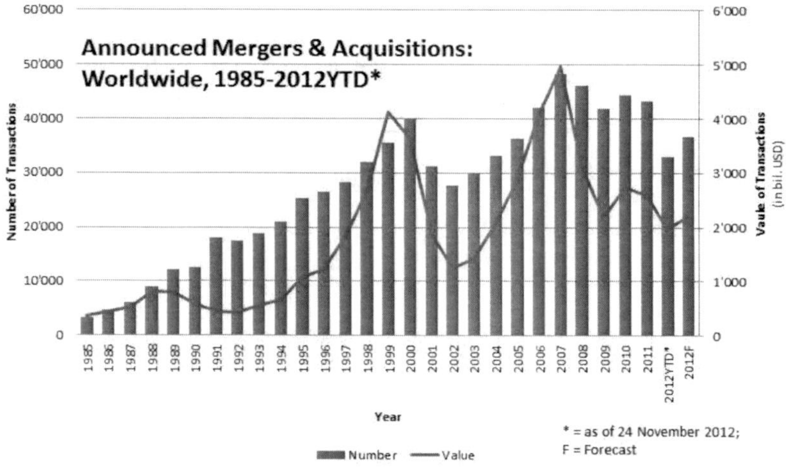

Figure 1: Announced Mergers & Acquisitions Worldwide 1985-2012. Source: http://www.imaa-institute.org/statistics-mergers-acquisitions.html#MergersAcquisitions_Worldwide

But why do those restructurings happen?

According to the current academic opinion, the main goal of mergers and acquisitions is to increase a company's power in the market and to achieve synergy effects. Instead of growing "naturally", companies tend to look for shortcuts to increase their (shareholder) value – they are pursuing "value capturing" instead of "natural growth". Theoretically, mergers and acquisitions also allow to create additional value by combining two companies – finance specialists refer to this phenomenon as "1+1=3". (Krusche, (2010) p. 13-16)

2.2 Definition of Mergers and Acquisitions

A merger is defined as a combination of assets by two previously separate firms into a new single legal entity. (Farschtschian, (2011) p. 32)

There are different forms of mergers. A *statutory merger* is a restructuring, in which only one company survives and the merged company ceases to exist. The acquiring company assumes all assets and liabilities of the merged company. A *subsidiary merger* is a consolidation of two companies where the merged company does not go out of existence, but is incorporated into the acquiring company as a subsidiary. A merger differs from a *consolidation,* in which two or more companies join to form a new entity and only the new entity survives. (Gaughan, (2010) p. 12-13)

Another term commonly heard is *takeover.* This term is more vague. Sometimes it can refer to a *friendly* acquisition, sometimes to a *hostile* one. (Gaughan, (2010) p. 13) These two general types of acquisitions need to be distinguished. When the board of directors of the target company agrees to an acquisition, this acquisition would be referred to as a friendly one. The managers of the target firm will typically keep their positions in the newly created entity. In contrast to that, a hostile acquisition (or takeover) is characterized by the acquired company trying to resist acquisition by others. They are undertaken against the will of the target company. (Farschtschian, (2011) p. 35) In the case of a hostile acquisition, managers of the acquired entity may lose their jobs after the acquisition. (Schnitzer, (1996) p. 37)

As a matter of fact, the actual number of mergers in mergers and acquisitions is small. Complete acquisitions account for more than 50 % of all M & A activity. Even when mergers are communicated between equal partners, in reality most result in one party dominating the other. As a matter of fact, the number of real, equal mergers is insignificant. (Farschtschian, (2011) p. 35; Peng, (2008) p. 273)

2.3 Types of Mergers and Acquisitions

Mergers can be categorized as horizontal, vertical or conglomerate. Each type has its own characteristics. (Gaughan, (2010) p. 13)

A combination of two businesses is referred to as a *horizontal merger.* The merger of Exxon and Mobil in 1998, or the combination of Pfizer and Wyeth in 2009, are typical examples of horizontal mergers. Horizontal mergers may lead to anticompetitive effects if the merger leads to a combined firm with increased market power. This is why horizontal mergers may be opposed on antitrust grounds. In recent years, the United States government seemed to be somewhat more liberal in allowing horizontal mergers than the European commission, which has traditionally been cautious when encountering potentially anticompetitive mergers. (Gaughan, (2010) p. 13-14)

This paper is going to investigate the significance of market power for M & A transactions later on.

A combination of two companies that are connected by a buyer-seller relationship is referred to as a *vertical merger.* (Gaughan, (2010) p. 14) More specifically, there are two categories of vertical M & A, namely *forward integration* (e.g. the acquirer buys a distributor) and *backward integration* (e.g. the acquirer buys a supplier of materials). (Brealey and Myers, (2003) p. 931-932) One example of a forward integrating vertical merger is the 1993 acquisition of Medco Containment Services, a marketer of prescription medicines by Merck, one of the world's largest drug producers. (Gaughan, (2010) p. 14) However, this specific acquisition was not very successful because consumers were concerned about drug producers' influence on consumer drug choice. (Gaughan, (2010) p. 14)

A merger where the companies are not competitors and do not have a buyer-seller relationship is referred to as a *conglomerate merger.* One example are the acquisitions of General Foods (1985), Kraft (1988) and Nabisco (2000) by Philip Morris. Due to the steadily declining US tobacco market, Philip Morris used the cash flows from its tobacco business to become less of a tobacco and more of a food company. Eventually, the company decided though, that the litigation problems of its US tobacco business were bad for its stock price and disassembled the conglomerate. (Gaughan, (2010) p. 14)

Another good example is General Electric, one of the few companies that has been able to successfully manage a diverse portfolio of businesses over a long time. (Gaughan, (2010) p. 14)

2.4 Objectives of Mergers and Acquisitions

The most obvious objective of an acquisition is normally *growth and expansion* of the acquiring company's assets, sales and market share. However, this is merely an intermediate objective. A more important objective may be the creation of sustainable competitive advantage, which leads to an enhancement of shareholders' wealth. (Sudarsanam, (1995) p. 1) Acquiring a target in a line of business or area into which the company may want to expand can be much faster than internal expansion. (Gaughan, (2010) p. 127)

An acquisition of a company may also provide certain *synergistic benefits* for the acquirer. In the pursuit of expansion, firms engaging in M & As cite potential synergy as one of the main reasons fort he transaction. Synergy occurs when the sum of the parts is more productive and valuable than the individual components by themselves. (Gaughan, (2010) p. 15; Krusche, (2010) p. 13-17)

Financial factors motivate some M & As. An acquirers' analysis may reveal, that the target is undervalued by the market. Certain buyers, such as private equity firms, may acquire undervalued targets to sell them shortly afterwards for a profit. (Gaughan, (2010) p. 15)

According to the managerial utility theory, acquisitions may also be driven by *managerial ego or desire for power.* (Sudarsanam, (1995) p. 1)

The importance of the factors that give rise to M & A activity varies, but whatever the fundamental objective of a specific M & A activity is, such activity must be part of the business and corporate strategies of the acquirer. (Sudarsanam, (1995) p. 1)

3 Motives for Engaging in M & A Activity

Mergers and Acquisitions are not strategies themselves (Marks and Mirvis, (2010) p. 6) however, they play a significant role in the involved companies' corporate or business strategies. Each acquisition or sale of an entity should be part of an overall strategy. It should be the result of a strategic necessity of all involved companies, which cannot be realized in a better way. (Kummer, Eiffe, Mölzer, (2011) p. 17) Typically, there is not going to be any M & A activity without plausible strategic reasoning. (Kummer, Eiffe, Mölzer, (2011) p. 17)

Before examining the various motives for M & A transactions, the general planning process for mergers and acquisitions shall be explained.

After that, possible M & A motives shall be distinguished.

Because value created for shareholders is one of the major variables companies are judged on, this paper is going to draw on this variable as a general framework for the distinction of M & A motives by asking – "What effect do motives have on the value created for shareholders?" and separating them into motives with positive, negative and neutral effect on shareholder value.

3.1 Planning M & A Activity

Each M & A transaction starts with internal preparations in the acquiring company and studies and analysis of the target company, its market and possibilities for development. (Picot, (2008) p. 27) In this planning phase, there are a few main aspects that need to be considered.

Should M & A activity be considered? This question mainly tries to determine the goals of a company and to answer the question, whether those goals can be achieved through M & A activity. The consequences of this question should be examined critically. (Picot, (2008) p. 27)

When should M & A activity take place? The question when M & A activity should ideally take place can only be answered by examining the company's strategic needs as well as its financial possibilities. (Picot, (2008) p. 27-28) Looking at macro-level economic events and trying to determine what state of a cycle the M & A market is currently in can also help companies save money. (Kummer, Eiffe, Mölzer, (2011) p. 3) If there are several M & A options and possibilities for a company, putting them in order from most- to least important can help making the right decision. (Picot, (2008) p. 28)

How should M & A activity happen? This question tries to examine which forms of M & A would be suitable for the specific situation. The different transactions that could be considered are typically mere cooperations, strategic alliances, acquiring a majority of a targets stock or acquiring the whole company. (Picot, (2008) p. 29)

Whenever answering these questions, executives should also consider how the company would fare in the future without the acquisition in question. (Picot, (2008) p. 30)

3.2 Distinction of M & A Motives by their Effect on Shareholder Value

The first and foremost task of a general manager is to deliver the results investors expect, through the effective operation of the business. Investors do not usually reward managers for merely achieving the expected results, but they will punish management if it falls short of expectations. One possibility for managers to meet or exceed investors' expectations is to pursue M & A activity. (Christensen et al., (2011) p. 50) There are two general reasons to acquire a company, which managers often confuse. (Christensen et al., (2011) p. 50)

The first one is to *boost a businesses' current performance,* which means holding on to a premium market position or cutting costs. This kind of acquisition often fails to help a company exceed its expected results, because investors anticipate and discount the possible performance improvements. (Christensen et al., (2011) p. 51-52)

The second one is to *reinvent a company's business model* and thereby fundamentally change the path of the business. Most executives do not understand how to identify the right targets to achieve that goal, how much to pay for them and how to integrate them into the acquiring company. And yet, they are the ones that typically pay off and help a business to exceed expected results. (Christensen et al., (2011) p. 54)

Regardless of the plans executives have for the further development of a business, *shareholder value* will always be essential when making a decision.

This section shall, at first, investigate the transaction motives, which may increase shareholder value. Motives, which decrease shareholder value or have an uncertain effect on shareholder value, shall be investigated after that.

3.2.1 Motives that increase Shareholder Value

These motives are generally considered to be the synergy effect, the achievement of economies of scope and –scale, increased market power and growth and the improvement of managerial efficiency.

3.2.1.1 Synergy

Searching for synergy is a crucial part of every phase of M & A activity, from translating strategy to objectives, to searching for a target, planning and integration. (Marks and Mirvis, (2010) p. 10) Generally, the expected synergy effects determine the price a company is willing to pay for an acquisition. Without considering these effects, an acquirer will normally not be willing to pay the price expected by the management of the company to be acquired. (Kummer, Eiffe, Mölzer, (2011) p. 31)

There are various types of possible synergies. According to Kummer, Eiffe, Mölzer ((2011) p. 32), cost-, collusive- and financial synergy are three crucial examples of synergies.

- **Cost Synergy**

Cost synergies are typically a result of cost optimization through integration. In order to correctly evaluate possible cost synergies, companies should try to quantify them and determine how likely they are going to take place. Cost synergies can be created in various parts of a business, such as administration, purchasing, logistics, information technology (IT), production and others. (Kummer, Eiffe, Mölzer, (2011) p. 33-34)

- **Collusive Synergy**

Collusive synergy refers to the gathering of scarce resources in order to increase market power and turnover and minimize risks at the same time. The value that collusive synergy generates for a company is potentially higher than the value yielded by cost- or financial synergy. (Chatterjee, (1986) p. 121)

- **Financial Synergy**

Financial synergy is the effect that is achieved when two formerly unrelated companies combine their capital. This combination will typically lead to a reduction in the cost of capital and a higher cash flow. (Chatterjee, (1986) p. 121) Another source of financial synergy are the potential savings of taxes on investment income and other tax benefits depending on the jurisdiction in which the transaction takes place. (Kummer, Eiffe, Mölzer, (2011) p. 35)

Some scholars claim that financial synergy is so important, under certain circumstances, without it there would be no advantage from a merger at all. (Fluck and Lynch, (1998) p. 22)

3.2.1.2 Economies of Scale or Scope

When long run average total costs decline as the quantity of output increases, there are said to be economies of scale. (Mankiw, (2011) p. 272) Firms in the same industry often merge in search of economies of scale. (Taylor and Weerapana, (2011) p. 212) Their goal in horizontal or conglomerate mergers is to share central services, such as office management, accounting, financial controlling and top-level management. (Brealey and Myers, (2003) p. 931)

In this case, cost reduction is not restricted only to horizontal mergers, but can also apply to other types of mergers. Vertical integration, with the goal of tightly integrating the production chain, for example, may lead to lower production costs. (Mueller, (1980) p. 30) Avoiding costs of communication and bargaining can also achieve cost advantages. (Ali-Yrkkö, (2002) p. 17)

Mergers are a way for firms with different types of skills to combine their knowledge and widen the scope of what they produce. Firms that achieve this goal are said to have economies of scope. (Taylor and Weerapana, (2011) p. 212-213) Companies may find outsourcing of certain activities efficient. Since this happens through acquiring a supplier or customer, economies of scope are typically achieved in vertical mergers and acquisitions. (Brealey and Myers, (2003) p. 931)

Although economies of scale and economies of scope can result in value creation for companies, firms should be aware of diseconomies of scale and –scope. These may result from diffusion of control, ineffective communication and the complexity of monitoring a new entity. (Sudarsanam, (2003) p. 108)

3.2.1.3 Increased Market Power and Growth

As already mentioned above, the most obvious objective of an acquisition is normally growth and expansion. (Sudarsanam, (1995) p. 1) This motive is also one, which typically increases shareholder value.

Market power exists, when a company is able to sell its goods or services above competitive levels of prices or when a company's costs are below levels of its competitors. Since exercising market power requires a company to have certain resources and capabilities, but also a certain size, many mergers and acquisitions are designed to achieve greater market power through buying a competitor, supplier or distributor to reach the size needed to fully leverage a company's resources and capabilities and gain competitive advantage in a market. (Ghosh Ray, (2010) p. 336)

Once a company has increased its market power, the financial position of the company will be strengthened. A stronger financial position will lead to increased profitability and also to increased shareholder value. (Sudarsanam, (2003) p. 214)

3.2.1.4 Managerial Efficiency

The theory of increased managerial efficiency through M & A activity follows the efficiency theory, which states that more efficient firms will acquire less efficient firms and thus realize gains. (Dash, (2010) p. 56)

This theory may also be applied to the market of corporate control. There, it states, that since potential bidders may pose a threat to executives' positions and monitor their performance closely, executives will improve managerial efficiency to avoid being dismissed after an M & A transaction. (Alchian and Demsetz, (1972) p. 777) Improved managerial efficiency can potentially lead to higher returns for shareholders.

Although M & A transactions may not be the only way of improving managerial efficiency, they tend to be among the fastest and most practical methods. (Brealey and Myers, (2003) p. 933)

3.2.2 Motives that decrease Shareholder Value

While companies usually aim to increase shareholder value by pursuing M & A activity, some motives for engaging in those transactions may actually lead to a decrease in shareholder value. Among those motives are managerial hubris, agency problems and the free cash flow theory.

3.2.2.1 Managerial Hubris

Managerial hubris are a term for the misconception that managers have about their own skill and talent, leading them to believe that they are capable of obtaining gains through the acquisition of a company when this is not the case. (Amihud and Miller, (1998) p. 71)

Managerial hubris can lead executives to ignore relevant information, which would have prevented a transaction if it had been known. Inadequate due diligence due to managerial hubris can also lead companies to pay excessive premiums to acquire a target. Ensuring dynamic due diligence and not tying fees paid to advisors to the acquisition price, can help companies avoid problems caused by managerial hubris. (Hitt, Harrison, Ireland, (2001) p. 178)

3.2.2.2 Agency Problems

Many of the reasons that let M & A transactions fail, are based on managerial conflicts of interest, so called agency problems. (Hitt, Harrison, Ireland, (2001) p. 165)

As already stated earlier in this paper, engaging in mergers and acquisitions may reduce possible risks to executives' careers and provide them with more discretion in their jobs. Self-centered behavior of executives is referred to as agency problems, because managers are supposed to operate as agents of the shareholders. If, instead of maximizing return to shareholders and stakeholders, personal issues of executives are the primary reasons for engaging in M & A transactions, these activities can be considered unethical and will typically lead to decreases in shareholder value. (Hitt, Harrison, Ireland, (2001) p. 165)

3.2.2.3 Free Cash Flow Theory

The free cash flow theory suggests that managers will use free cash flow to invest in mergers that have negative net present values in order to build corporate empires, from which they will derive personal benefits. Those benefits may include enhanced job security and increased compensation. (Jensen, (1986b) p. 323-329; Megginson and Smart, (2008) p. 868)

Citing the oil industry of the 1970s, Jensen ((1986b) p. 323-329) concludes that excess free cash flow and investment in transactions, that do not benefit a company but only its managers, result in destruction of shareholder value.

3.2.3 Motives with uncertain impact on Shareholder Value

- **Diversification**

The basic idea of corporate diversification and conglomerate mergers is that the combination of two businesses, with cash flows that are not correlated, will create a firm with less volatile cash flows and significantly lower business risk, because bad results in one business can theoretically be offset by good results in another business. (Megginson and Smart, (2008) p. 868-869)

Diversification supporters claim, that less volatile cash flows make a company less risky and thus lower the required return on debt and that the internal capital markets created by a conglomerate merger enable companies to fund the “rising star” businesses with money from its own “cash cow” businesses. Since this financing happens internally, riskier business ventures can be financed with “cheaper” capital, enabling a company to engage in potentially profitable new markets more easily. (Megginson and Smart, (2008) p. 869)

Further research on diversification and conglomerate mergers showed, however, that those transactions are not likely to result in any synergies other than financial and that the net effect of conglomerate mergers is zero wealth creation. Furthermore, internal capital markets turned out to result in severe agency problems. (Megginson and Smart, (2008) p. 869)

For a considerable amount of time, diversification was actually considered a motive that enhances shareholder value. But over the time, the capital markets have learned of the failure of diversification strategies. This applies specifically to unrelated diversification. Due to these empirical findings and due to further research on the topic, diversification is now considered to have uncertain impact on shareholder value. (Megginson and Smart, (2008) p. 869; Peng, (2008) p. 256-272)

4 Summary and How to Make M & A Transactions Successful

As already mentioned earlier, every new wave of mergers and acquisitions sets new records in transaction volume and in the amount of M & A transactions. Acquisitions are a quick way for a company to grow and often very rewarding. (Hitt, Harrison, Ireland, (2001) p. 177) However, they are prone to failure and many of them go wrong. (Hitt, Harrison, Ireland, (2001) p. 177)

After reviewing and summarizing the main reasons for companies to pursue M & A transactions, this chapter shall give an overview of how to avoid the most common mistakes that may be made under aforementioned motives.

- **The Creation of Synergy**

There are various forms of synergy, but they all have four foundations in common. The four foundations of the creation of synergy are *strategic fit, organizational fit, managerial actions* and *value creation.* (Hitt, Harrison, Ireland, (2001) p. 180)

The effective matching of organizational capabilities of two companies is referred to as *strategic fit*. Different types of strategic fit can be found in various areas of a company, such as research and development (R & D), management or marketing. Although no two companies are exactly equal, similar management processes, cultures, systems and structures can facilitate communication, learning and sharing activities. This type of fit is referred to as *organizational fit.* *Managerial actions* are needed to take advantage of those two types of fit and to facilitate the creation of synergy. In order to achieve this as efficiently as possible, a company should ensure effective knowledge sharing between executives and may engage in executive transfers across companies. After all, *value creation* can only take place if the benefits drawn from synergy exceed the costs for developing and exploiting it. (Hitt, Harrison, Ireland, (2001) p. 180; Chatterjee et al., (1992) p. 319)

- **Due Diligence and Friendliness**

Many mergers have failed because of inadequate due diligence. Managerial hubris are often one of the main causes of a lack of due diligence. Executives overestimate their experience and understanding of an industry and lead companies into engaging in deals that would not have been made if relevant information had been known. Excessive premiums paid for acquiring a firm are typical results of a lack of due diligence as well. Executives should try to avoid managerial hubris and ensure a dynamic due diligence process for every M & A transaction a company engages in. Due diligence should involve an analysis of all characteristics of a possible target firm, such as its financial condition, tangible and intangible assets and management. As already mentioned before, fees paid to advisors should not be tied to the purchase price, as this may lead to wrong incentives. (Hitt, Harrison, Ireland, (2001) p. 178-179)

Friendliness can also dramatically benefit an M & A transaction. Target firm resistance, or misunderstandings between managers of the acquiring- and the target firm can potentially destroy value by making the transfer of information during the acquisition process and the ensuing integration of a target firm more complicated and possibly increasing the premium paid for a company. Executives involved in an M & A transaction should announce the new management team early and keep in close contact with all stakeholders involved in a transaction. The "we win – you lose" mentality, which is found so frequently in acquisitions, should be avoided as well. (Hitt, Harrison, Ireland, (2001) p. 178-179)

- **Relatedness of Companies**

One popular view is, that the acquisition of businesses that differ in fundamental ways can lead to financial synergy through reduced risk and higher returns. However, actual M & A transactions have shown, that these outcomes are difficult to obtain from acquisitions unrelated to a company's core business. In many cases, cultural and management differences are big and they can be magnified if firms are not related. The financial markets view unrelated acquisitions unfavorably and many of them are divested shortly after their purchase. The result of all these problems is that positive benefits from financial synergy are typically not strong enough to offset the negative effects of diversification. Acquisitions related to the firms core business are more likely to be successful. (Hitt, Harrison, Ireland, (2001) p. 181)

- **Ethical Concerns**

There is probably no other factor that can limit the success of M & A more than ethical problems. Incorrect, misleading or deceptive information is among the greatest risks associated with all types of transactions. One of the major sources of that kind of risks are unethical actions carried out by managers, who sometimes give too much weight to their own personal interests. Those kinds of actions are usually carried out at the expense of the shareholders and stakeholders of all companies involved in a transaction. Conflicts of interest and managerial hubris can lead to unnecessary layoffs and poor acquisition performance. (Hitt, Harrison, Ireland, (2001) p. 181; Werhane, (1988) p. 41-42) Companies, and especially their boards of directors, should develop incentives that encourage executives to make decisions that are ethically correct and beneficial to the whole company and all stakeholders involved in an M & A transaction. (Hitt, Harrison, Ireland, (2001) p. 181)

References

Alchian, Armen; Demsetz, Harold. *Production, Information Costs and Economic Organization*, American Economic Review, 62, 5, 777-795. 1972.

Ali-Yrkkö, Jyrki. *Mergers and acquisitions: Reason and results.* ETLA Discussion Papers, The Research Institute of the Finnish Economy (ETLA), No. 792. 2002.

Amihud, Yakov; Miller, Geoffrey. *Bank Mergers & Acquisitions.* Springer, New York, NY. 1998.

Brealey, Richard A.; Myers, Stewart C.. *Principles of Corporate Finance, 8th Edition.* McGraw-Hill, New York, NY. 2003.

Chatterjee, Sayan. *Types of Synergy and Economic Value: The impact of Acquisitions on Merging and Rival Firms.* Strategic Management Journal, 7, 119-139. 1986.

Chatterjee, Sayan; Lubatkin, Michael H.; Schweiger, David M.; Weber, Yaakov.. *Cultural differences and shareholder value in related mergers: Linking equity and human capital.* Strategic Management Journal, 13, 319-334. 1992.

Christensen, Clayton M.; Alton, Richard; Rising, Curtis; Waldeck, Andrew. *The New M & A Playbook – Why you should pay top dollar for a "killer deal" and other new rules for making acquisitions.* Harvard Business Review, March 2011: 48-57. 2011.

Copeland, Thomas E.; Weston, Fred J.; Shastri, Kuldeep. *Financial Theory and Corporate Policy.* Prentice Hall International, Hertfordshire (UK). 2004.

Dash, Ambika Prasad. *Mergers and Acquisitions.* I.K. International Publishing House Pvt. Ltd., New Delhi. 2010.

DePamphilis, Donald M.. *Mergers and acquisitions: All you need to know.* Elsevier, Oxford (UK). 2011.

Farschtschian, Farsam. *The Secret of Successful Acquisitions – Abandoning the Myth of Board Influence.* Campus Verlag, Frankfurt am Main. 2011.

Fluck, Zsuzsanna; Lynch, Anthony W.. *Why Do Firms Merge and Then Divest: A Theory of Financial Synergy.* NYU Stern School of Business, Department of Finance Working Paper Series, New York, NY. 1998.

Gaughan, Patrick A.. *Mergers, Acquisitions and Corporate Restructurings.* John Wiley & Sons, New York, NY. 2010.

Ghosh Ray, Kamal. *Mergers and Acquisitions.* PHI Learning Pvt. Ltd., New Delhi. 2010.

Hitt, Michael A.; Harrison, Jeffrey S.; Ireland R. Duane. *Mergers and Acquisitions: A Guide to Creating Value for Stakeholders.* Oxford University Press, New York, NY. 2001.

Homburg, Christian; Bucerius, Matthias. *Is speed of integration really a success factor of mergers and acquisitions? An analysis of the role of internal and external relatedness.* Strategic Management Journal, 27, 347-367. 2006.

Jensen, Michael. *Agency Costs of Free Cash Flow, Corporate Finance and Takeovers.* American Economic Review, 76, 323-329. 1986b.

Kummer, Christopher; Eiffe, Franz Ferdinand; Mölzer, Wolfgang. *Mergers & Acquisitions Leitfaden zum Kauf & Verkauf von Unternehmen.* LexisNexis, Wien. 2011.

Krusche, Bernhard. *Merger? Merger! Fusionsprozesse verstehen und gestalten.* Carl-Auer Verlag, Heidelberg. 2010.

Mankiw, Gregory N.. *Principles of Economics.* Cengage Learning, Stamford, CT. 2011.

Marks, Mitchell Lee; Mirvis, Philipp H.. *Joining Forces – Making One Plus One Equal Three in Mergers, Acquisitions and Alliances.* Jossey-Bass, San Francisco, CA. 2010.

Megginson, William L.; Smart, Scott B.. *Introduction to Corporate Finance.* Cengage Learning, Stamford, CT. 2008.

Mueller, Dennis C.. *The Determinants and Effects of Mergers: International Comparison.* Oelgeschlager, Gunn & Hain, Cambridge, MA. 1980.

Peng, Mike W.. *Global Strategy.* Cengage Learning, Stamford CT. 2008.

Picot, Gerhard. *Handbuch Mergers & Acquisitions Planung – Durchführung – Integration.* Schäffer-Poeschel Verlag, Stuttgart. 2008.

Schnitzer, Monika. *Hostile versus friendly takeovers*. Economica, 63, No. 249, 37-55. 1996.

Sudarsanam, Sudi. *The essence of mergers and acquisitions.* Prentice Hall International, Hertfordshire (UK). 1995.

Sudarsanam, Sudi. *Creating Value Through Mergers and Acquisitions: The Challenges, an Integrated and International Perspective.* Prentice Hall, Upper Saddle River, NJ. 2003.

Taylor, John B.; Weerapana, Akila. *Principles of Economics.* Cengage Learning, Stamford, CT. 2011.

Werhane, Patricia H.. *Two Ethical Issues in Mergers and Acquisitions.* Journal of Business Ethics, 7, 41-45. 1988.